HAYNER r

RECEIVED JUL 0 5 2013 BY

Y0-BRM-746

Stepping into Standards
Theme Series

Rain Forest Adventures

Written by
Kimberly Jordano and Tebra Corcoran

Editor: Teri L. Fisch
Illustrator: Darcy Tom
Cover Illustrator: Kimberly Schamber
Designer: Moonhee Pak
Cover Designer: Moonhee Pak
Art Director: Tom Cochrane
Project Director: Carolea Williams

No Longer the Property of
Hayner Public Library District

HAYNER PUBLIC LIBRARY DISTRICT
ALTON, ILLINOIS

OVERDUES 10 PER DAY, MAXIMUM FINE
COST OF ITEM
ADDITIONAL $5.00 SERVICE CHARGE
APPLIED TO
LOST OR DAMAGED ITEMS

© 2003 Creative Teaching Press, Inc., Huntington Beach, CA 92649
Reproduction of activities in any manner for use in the classroom and not for commercial sale is permissible.
Reproduction of these materials for an entire school or for a school system is strictly prohibited.

Table of Contents

Introduction

Due to the often-changing national, state, and district standards, it is often difficult to "squeeze in" fascinating topics for student enrichment on top of meeting required standards and including a balanced program in your classroom curriculum. The *Stepping into Standards Theme Series* will help you incorporate required subjects and skills for your kindergarten and first-grade children while engaging them in a fun theme. Children will participate in a variety of language arts experiences to help them with **phonemic awareness** and **reading** and **writing** skills. They will also have fun with **math activities, hands-on science activities,** and **social studies class projects.**

The creative lessons in *Rain Forest Adventures* provide imaginative, innovative ideas to help you motivate children as you turn your classroom into a tropical rain forest. The activities will inspire children to explore the rain forest as well as provide them with opportunities to enhance their knowledge and meet standards.

Invite children to "trek" into a tropical rain forest as they
- participate in phonemic awareness activities that feature theme-related poems
- create mini-books that reinforce guided reading and sight word practice
- contribute to shared and independent reading and writing experiences about rain forest animals
- practice counting and addition with peanut monkeys
- investigate how animals use camouflage for survival
- compare and contrast their own lives with the lives of people who live in the rain forest
- complete several fun art projects as they turn their room into a rain forest
- participate in a rain forest culminating event to showcase their work

Each resource book in the *Stepping into Standards Theme Series* includes standards information, easy-to-use reproducibles, and a full-color overhead transparency to help you integrate a fun theme into your required curriculum. You will see how easy it can be to incorporate creative activities with academic requirements while children enjoy their adventures in the rain forest!

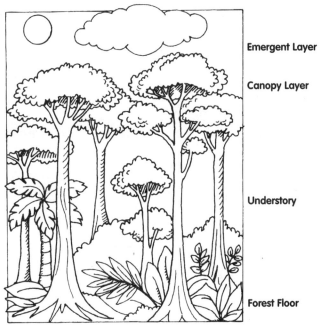

Emergent Layer

Canopy Layer

Understory

Forest Floor

Meeting Standards

Language Arts

Skill	Find Your Monkey, page 7	Carly Crocodile, page 7	Colorful Iguanas, page 11	I Live in the Rain Forest, page 11	Reading Aloud, page 14	Morning Message, page 15	My Monkey, page 16	Pocket Chart Stories, page 16	Sentence Puzzle, page 16	Day and Night in the Jungle mini-book, page 19	The Greedy Python mini-book, page 23	Safari Sleep Over Fun, page 27	A Safari Guide's Adventure, page 28	Rain Forest Word Bank, page 31	Rain Forest Question of the Week, page 31	Meet the Safari Guides, page 32	Gorilla Facts and Fiction, page 32	Write a Rhyme, page 34	Did You Know?, page 34	Piranhas, page 35	In the Rain Forest, page 35	Safari Guide, page 38	Marvelous Monkeys, page 40
Phonemic Awareness																							
Identify beginning consonant sounds	•	•																					
Identify letters	•																						
Identify rhyming words			•	•														•					
Isolate beginning sounds	•	•																					
Recognize rhythm and rhyme			•	•			•											•					
Substitute beginning consonant sounds	•																						
Reading																							
Apply phonics concepts							•			•	•	•	•										
Apply reading strategies				•	•	•	•	•		•	•	•	•								•	•	•
Develop awareness of concepts of print						•	•	•	•		•		•	•	•	•	•	•					
Develop oral language skills	•		•	•		•	•	•	•	•	•	•	•	•	•	•	•	•					
Identify plot, characters, conflict, and resolution					•																		
Improve reading comprehension											•	•	•										
Improve reading fluency							•				•		•	•	•	•	•						
Improve story comprehension					•						•	•					•			•			
Make predictions					•																		
Recognize sight word vocabulary						•	•	•	•	•	•	•	•	•	•	•	•	•			•	•	•
Track words from left to right						•	•	•	•	•	•	•	•	•	•	•	•	•			•		
Writing																							
Apply phonics skills						•				•	•			•	•	•	•	•	•	•	•	•	•
Brainstorm and organize ideas														•	•	•	•	•	•	•	•	•	•
Choose correct punctuation						•										•	•		•		•		•
Develop focused, detailed writing																					•	•	
Follow spelling rules						•				•	•			•		•	•	•	•	•	•	•	•
Incorporate letter and word spacing						•				•	•			•	•	•	•	•	•	•	•	•	•
Model letter formation						•								•	•	•	•		•		•		
Model sentence structure						•								•	•	•	•		•				
Practice correct letter formation						•				•	•				•				•	•	•	•	•
Write complete sentences														•						•	•		•

Meeting Standards

Math / Science / Social Studies

	Rain Forest Treat Tote, page 42	Animal Quilt Glyph, page 44	Peanut Monkey Math, page 47	Interactive Monkey Math Poem, page 47	Addition Tree Frog, page 49	Beetle Bug Clock, page 49	Camouflage Tree Frogs, page 51	Plant a Jungle Garden, page 51	Rain Forest Birds Like to Eat, page 52	Rain Forest Guessing Bucket, page 55	Rain Forest People, page 55	Save the Rain Forest Bookmaking, page 57	Rain Forest Event, page 58	Binoculars, page 58	Safari Sack, page 59	The Large Python, page 59	Yummy Food Recipes, page 59	Large Rain Forest Tree, page 60	Safari Snack Shack, page 60	Sunset Jungle Cruise Bulletin Board, page 61	Waterfall and Piranha Pond Bulletin Board, page 61
Math																					
Add			•		•	•															
Analyze data	•	•							•												
Count	•	•	•	•	•	•															
Count using one-to-one correspondence		•	•		•																
Graph	•																				
Make patterns		•															•				
Measure ingredients																	•				
Subtract					•	•															
Tell time								•													
Use money																			•		
Write numbers correctly	•		•	•	•												•				
Science																					
Collect data							•	•	•												
Experiment and investigate									•												
Make observations							•	•	•												
Understand how animals' characteristics help them survive							•		•												
Use scientific inquiry							•		•												
Social Studies																					
Compare and contrast cultures												•									
Practice reusing and recycling													•								
Understand the importance of products grown or made in a region											•		•								
Understand why environmental protection is important													•								
Use clues to identify a product												•									
Additional Language Arts																					
Apply reading strategies	•		•															•	•		
Develop oral language skills		•		•								•		•					•		
Follow spelling rules					•							•				•				•	•
Follow step-by-step directions		•															•		•	•	
Improve story comprehension				•					•	•	•	•									
Incorporate letter and word spacing	•							•				•		•		•	•			•	•
Practice correct letter formation	•		•					•				•		•		•	•			•	•
Recognize rhythm and rhyme				•																	
Write complete sentences								•			•						•			•	•

Instant Learning Environment

This resource includes a full-color overhead transparency of a rain forest environment that can be used in a variety of ways to enhance the overall theme of the unit and make learning more interactive. Simply place the transparency on an overhead projector, and shine it against a blank wall, white butcher paper, or a white sheet. Then, choose an idea from the list below, or create your own ideas for using this colorful backdrop.

Unit Introduction

Give children clues about the rain forest unit. For example, say *We are going to study about a habitat. It is usually hot and it has a lot of rain. It has many trees, plants, and animals.* Invite children to use the clues to discuss what the unit might be about. Then, display the transparency to give children a quick overview of the environment and an introduction to the unit.

Or, cut out puzzle pieces from an 8½" x 11" (21.5 cm x 28 cm) sheet of paper. Place the puzzle pieces on top of the transparency on the overhead projector so they cover it entirely. Turn on the projector. None of the rain forest environment will show. Remove one puzzle piece at a time, and describe the uncovered section. Invite children to identify the environment. Then, continue to remove pieces, asking children to predict what they might see next until you have revealed the entire transparency.

Dramatic Play

Use the transparency as a backdrop for children to perform the dramatic play described on page 28. Have children wear a character headband (glue cutouts from the Props reproducible on page 30 to sentence strips) as they perform.

Math Practice

Create addition and subtraction story problems. Project the transparency on a blank wall, and place clear colored chips on the overhead projector to represent animals in different layers of the rain forest. Say a story problem about the picture. For example, place five chips in the emergent layer, and say *There are 5 macaws in the emergent layer and 2 fly away.* (remove 2 chips) *How many macaws are left?* Have children write a number sentence and use manipulatives to solve the problem.

Phonemic Awareness

ABC Find Your Monkey

MATERIALS

✓ Monkey reproducible (page 8)
✓ letter cutouts
✓ fishing line

Use this activity on the first day of your rain forest unit. Copy a Monkey reproducible for each child, and glue a letter cut-out of the first letter of his or her first name on the monkey's stomach (or write the letter in large, bold print). Hole-punch the monkeys, and hang them with fishing line. Invite children to walk into the classroom, find the monkey that has the same letter as the first letter of their name, and stand under it. Have them say the sound the letter makes and then say their name to assess letter and sound recognition. To extend the activity, have children stand under a different letter, say the sound the letter makes, and then say their name with this letter as the first sound.

ABC Carly Crocodile

MATERIALS

✓ Carly Crocodile Food Cards (page 9)
✓ "Carly Crocodile" poem (page 10)
✓ green construction paper
✓ paper bags

Copy and cut apart a class set of Carly Crocodile Food Cards. Copy the poem "Carly Crocodile" on green construction paper. Give each child a set of cards, a copy of the poem "Carly Crocodile," and a paper bag. Have children cut out the crocodile and glue it to their bag so its head is at the opening of the bag. Read aloud the poem, and invite children to "feed" Carly the foods that begin with c by placing them in their bag.

Monkey

Rain Forest Adventures © 2003 Creative Teaching Press

Carly Crocodile Food Cards

Rain Forest Adventures © 2003 Creative Teaching Press

Carly Crocodile

(read to the tune of "On Top of Old Smokey")

Meet Carly the Crocodile.
She munches on C's.
If she eats the wrong foods,
It might make her sneeze.
She munches on carrots
    and crackers, too!
What will you feed her
If she dines with you?

Rain Forest Adventures © 2003 Creative Teaching Press

Colorful Iguanas

Copy the poem "Colorful Iguanas" on construction paper, and then cut it out. Trace the iguana cutout on construction paper in assorted colors, and cut them out. Write the color of each iguana on its body. Hole-punch the head of the iguanas, and place them on a metal ring. Read aloud the poem, and insert a word that rhymes with a color (e.g., *bean*, *stink*) in the first blank. Invite children to say the correct rhyming color word (e.g., *green*, *pink*) to complete the last line of the poem. Hold up the matching iguana. Reread the poem several times with new sets of rhyming words.

MATERIALS

✓ "Colorful Iguanas" poem (page 12)
✓ construction paper
✓ metal ring

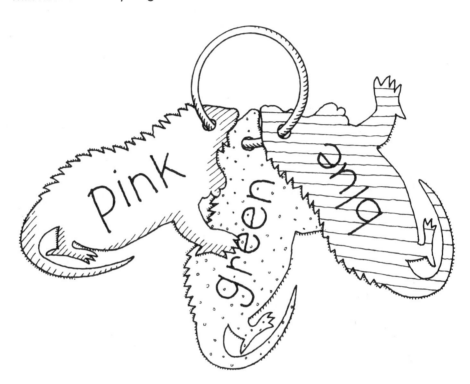

I Live in the Rain Forest

Copy the song "I Live in the Rain Forest" on construction paper. Make an enlarged copy of the Props reproducible and a copy of the Monkey reproducible on construction paper. Cut out a sloth, snake, and parrot, and cut out the monkey. Sing each verse. Have children identify the animal that matches the description and rhymes with the last word in the verse. Hold up the matching paper animal, or invite a child to hold it up.

MATERIALS

✓ "I Live in the Rain Forest" song (page 13)
✓ Props reproducible (page 30)
✓ Monkey reproducible (page 8)
✓ construction paper

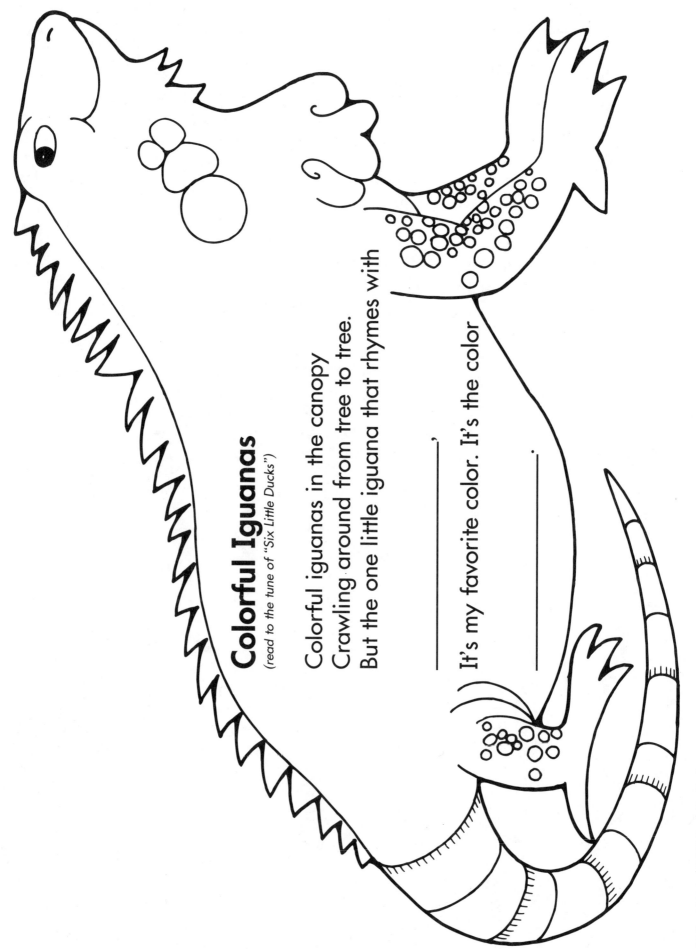

Colorful Iguanas
(read to the tune of "Six Little Ducks")

Colorful iguanas in the canopy
Crawling around from tree to tree.
But the one little iguana that rhymes with

_____,

It's my favorite color. It's the color

_____.

Rain Forest Adventures © 2003 Creative Teaching Press

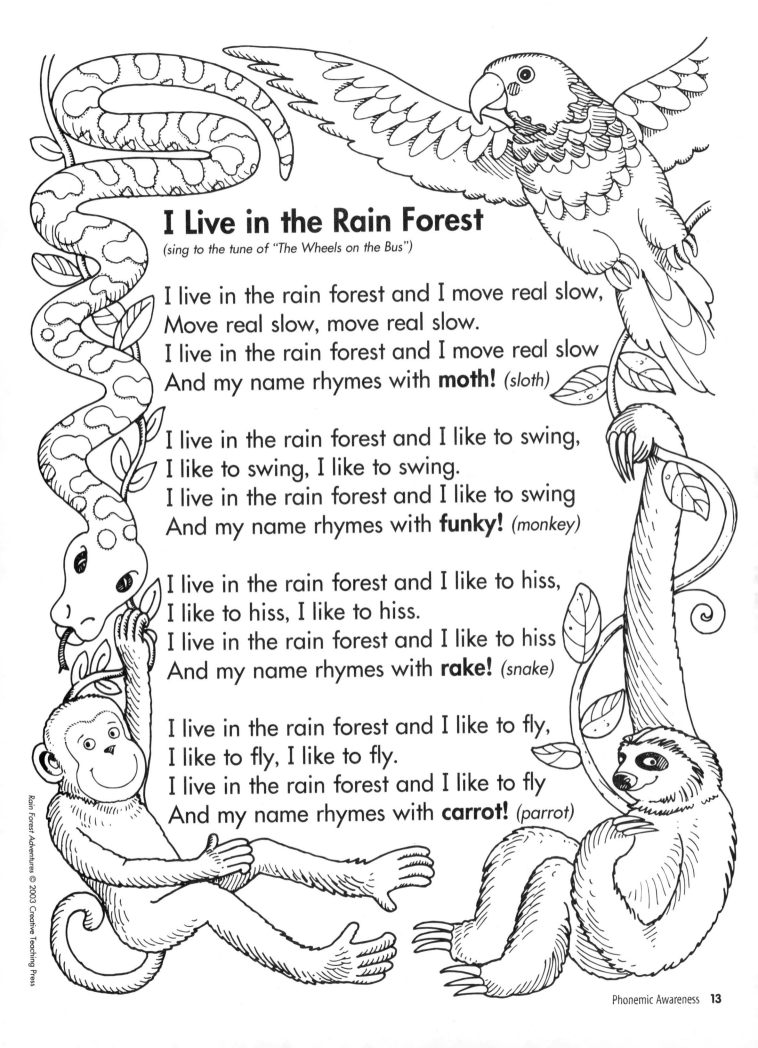

I Live in the Rain Forest

(sing to the tune of "The Wheels on the Bus")

I live in the rain forest and I move real slow,
Move real slow, move real slow.
I live in the rain forest and I move real slow
And my name rhymes with **moth!** *(sloth)*

I live in the rain forest and I like to swing,
I like to swing, I like to swing.
I live in the rain forest and I like to swing
And my name rhymes with **funky!** *(monkey)*

I live in the rain forest and I like to hiss,
I like to hiss, I like to hiss.
I live in the rain forest and I like to hiss
And my name rhymes with **rake!** *(snake)*

I live in the rain forest and I like to fly,
I like to fly, I like to fly.
I live in the rain forest and I like to fly
And my name rhymes with **carrot!** *(parrot)*

Rain Forest Adventures © 2003 Creative Teaching Press

Modeled Reading

Introduce the rain forest to your class by reading aloud books from the following literature list or others with similar content. Invite children to look at the book cover and pictures and discuss what they see. Ask them to predict what the book will be about and to point out animals, plants, and details that relate to the rain forest.

Literature List

The Big Yawn by Keith Faulkner (The Millbrook Press)

Crictor by Tomi Ungerer (Econo-Clad Books)

Crocodiles Yawn to Keep Cool by Kate Petty (Copper Beech Books)

Eye Wonder: Rain Forest by Elinor Greenwood (DK Publishing)

Flashy Fantastic Rain Forest Frogs by Dorothy Hinshaw Patent (Walker and Company)

Gorillas by Seymour Simon (HarperCollins)

Gorillas: Gentle Giants of the Forest by Joyce Milton (Random House)

The Great Kapok Tree: A Tale of the Amazon Rain Forest by Lynne Cherry (Voyager)

The Greedy Python by Richard Buckley (Little Simon)

The Grouchy Ladybug by Eric Carle (HarperCollins)

Here Is the Tropical Rain Forest by Madeleine Dunphy (Hyperion Press)

How Monkeys Make Chocolate: Foods and Medicines from the Rainforests by Adrian Forsyth (Owl Communications)

In the Rain Forest (The Magic School Bus) by Eva Moore (Scholastic)

People in the Rain Forest by Saviour Pirotta (Raintree Steck-Vaughn)

Piranhas by Mary Berendes (Child's World)

Rain Forest Babies by Kathy Darling (Econo-Clad Books)

The Rain Forest Counts! by Lisa McCourt (Troll Communications)

Rain Forest Ride by Julia Andrews (Scholastic)

Rain Forests by Joy Palmer (Raintree Steck-Vaughn)

Rainforest by Helen Cowcher (Milet Publishing)

Rainforest Birds by Bobbie Kalman (Crabtree Publishing)

Recycle! A Handbook for Kids by Gail Gibbons (Little, Brown and Company)

Red-Eyed Tree Frog by Joy Cowley (Scholastic)

Reduce, Reuse, Recycle by Rozanne Lanczak Williams (Creative Teaching Press)

A Shaman's Apprentice: A Tale of the Amazon Rain Forest by Lynne Cherry and Mark J. Plotkin (Gulliver Books)

Sloth's Shoes by Jeanne Willis (Red Fox)

Ten Sly Piranhas by William Wise (Penguin)

The Upside-Down Sloth by Fay Robinson (Children's Press)

A Walk in the Rainforest by Kristin Joy Pratt (Dawn Publications)

Where Does the Garbage Go? by Paul Showers (Scott Foresman)

Where the Forest Meets the Sea by Jeannie Baker (William Morrow & Company)

Willy the Wimp by Anthony Browne (Candlewick Press)

Shared Reading

Morning Message

M A T E R I A L S

✓ chart paper or dry erase board
✓ markers or dry erase markers
✓ Wikki Stix® (optional)
✓ reading stick

Turn your morning message into a "safari adventure"! This activity is a great way to introduce your new theme. Write a message (see sample below) on chart paper or a dry erase board each morning. As you write, invite children to help you sound out words, spell words, and decide what to write. Create a "secret code," and write a "secret message" for children to decode each day. Write the alphabet, and write a number above each letter (e.g., A–1, Z–26), or put numbers below your posted alphabet. Beneath the morning message, draw a blank and a number for each letter of the secret message (Look at the monkey).

Dear Safari Guides in Room ___.
Today is Friday, April ___, 200___.
Today we will begin to learn about the rain forest.
Can you read my code?

___   ___   ___   ___
12   15   15   11

___   ___   ___   ___   ___
1   20   20   8   5

___   ___   ___   ___   ___   ___ .
13   15   14   11   5   25

1	2	3	4	5	6	7
A	B	C	D	E	F	G
8	9	10	11	12	13	14
H	I	J	K	L	M	N
15	16	17	18	19	20	21
O	P	Q	R	S	T	U
22	23	24	25	26		
V	W	X	Y	Z		

Invite children to write in the room number and date with a marker or dry erase marker. Have them circle letters, words, or punctuation they know with a marker, a dry erase marker, or Wikki Stix. Depending on the level of the children, leave complete words or word chunks deleted for them to fill in. Have volunteers write the missing letters in the coded message. Have children read aloud the completed message. Choose a child to be the "safari guide of the day," and invite him or her to use a reading stick (see page 18) to track and reread the morning message.

My Monkey

M A T E R I A L S

✓ "My Monkey" poem
   (page 17)
✓ construction paper or
   overhead transparency
✓ reading stick

Write the poem "My Monkey" in large print, and glue it on the back of a large construction paper monkey head. Or, use the reproducible to make an overhead transparency. Read aloud the poem with children. Point to the words as you read them. Reread the poem, and have a volunteer use a reading stick (see page 18) to point to the words as the class reads them. To extend the activity, make a construction paper copy of the poem for each child. Encourage children to reread it independently, memorize it, and recite it for the class.

Pocket Chart Stories

M A T E R I A L S

✓ mini-book reproducibles
   (pages 19–22 and 23–26)
✓ sentence strips
✓ colored markers
✓ pocket chart
✓ sticky notes

Choose a mini-book, and write each sentence on a separate sentence strip. Highlight key words by writing them in a different color to help children easily recognize them. Place the sentence strips in a pocket chart. Make copies of the mini-book pictures, color them, and place each picture next to the matching sentence. Have the class read aloud the story while you track and stress high-frequency words. Invite the class to revisit the story. Select a word, letter, or part of a word, and cover it with a sticky note. Invite children to use reading strategies to identify the selected word. Remind them to look at the beginning sound and to decide if their answer makes sense in the sentence.

Sentence Puzzle

M A T E R I A L S

✓ sentence strips
✓ pocket chart

Choose a sentence strip from the pocket chart story (see above), and cut it apart to create word cards. Pass out the cards, and have children read aloud their word. Invite children with word cards to stand up and arrange their words so they form a sentence. Have them put the cards back in the pocket chart in the correct order.

My Monkey

(read to the tune of "My Bonnie Lies Over the Ocean")

My monkey swings in the jungle.
My monkey swings in the tree.
My monkey likes to be silly.
Oh, monkey please come play with me!

Rain Forest Adventures © 2003 Creative Teaching Press

Guided Reading

Assembling the Mini-Books and Reading Sticks

M A T E R I A L S

✓ mini-book reproducibles (pages 19–22 and 23–26)
✓ construction paper
✓ craft sticks
✓ stickers or small objects
✓ envelopes

Make single-sided copies of the reproducibles for each mini-book. Fold each page in half so the blank side of the paper does not show, and staple the pages inside a construction paper cover so that the creased sides face out. Use black construction paper for *Day and Night in the Jungle* and green construction paper for *The Greedy Python*.

Reading sticks help children with one-to-one correspondence and left-to-right directionality and are fun to use. To make a reading stick, glue to the end of a craft stick a sticker or small object that relates to the theme of the mini-book. For example, use a small plastic frog for *Day and Night in the Jungle* and a small snake for *The Greedy Python*. Seal envelopes, and cut them in half. Glue each envelope to the front inside cover of a mini-book to make a "pocket." Place a reading stick in the pocket.

Sight Word Practice

M A T E R I A L S

✓ assembled mini-books (see above)
✓ assembled reading sticks (see above)
✓ art supplies

After children review the mini-book text in a shared reading lesson (see page 16), have them write the missing sight words in the blanks to complete their mini-book. In *Day and Night in the Jungle*, the sight word is *here*. In *The Greedy Python*, the sight words are *ate* and *eat*. Invite children to decorate their covers and color the illustrations in their books. Have children use reading sticks to help them track words as they read the stories in guided reading groups.

Day and Night in the Jungle

by
Safari Guide

Dedicated to

2

Rain Forest Adventures © 2003 Creative Teaching Press

It's night in the jungle.

_____ come

the cats.

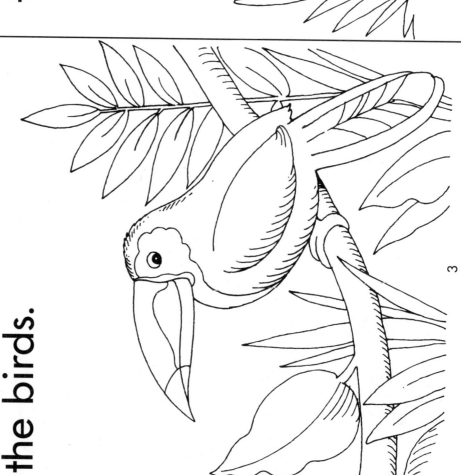

4

It's day in the jungle.

_____ come

the birds.

3

Rain Forest Adventures © 2003 Creative Teaching Press

It's day in the jungle.

come the
_____ monkeys.

5

It's night in the jungle.

come the
_____ tree frogs.

6

Rain Forest Adventures © 2003 Creative Teaching Press

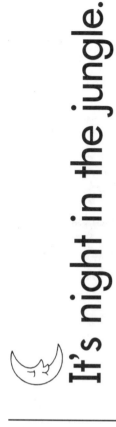

It's night in the jungle.

Please do not eat me!

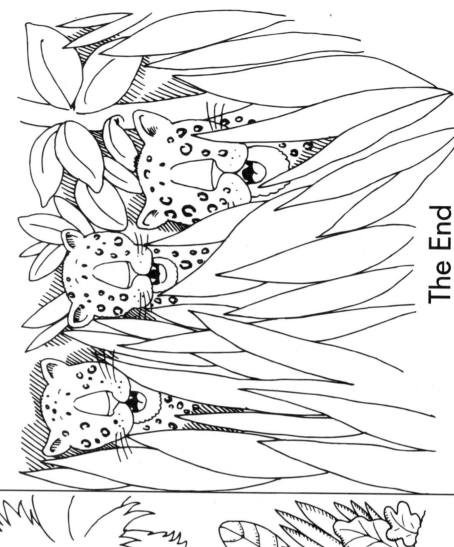

The End

8

It's day in the jungle,

so much to see!

7

Rain Forest Adventures © 2003 Creative Teaching Press

The Greedy Python

by
Safari Guide

Dedicated to

Rain Forest Adventures © 2003 Creative Teaching Press

The greedy python was

so hungry you see!

It _____ the butterfly,

But it didn't _____ me!

3

The greedy python was

so hungry you see!

It _____ the tree frog,

But it didn't _____ me!

4

Rain Forest Adventures © 2003 Creative Teaching Press

The greedy python was so
hungry you see!

It _____ the spider monkey,

But it didn't _____ me!

The greedy python was
so hungry you see!

It _____ the sloth,

But it didn't _____ me!

5

6

Rain Forest Adventures © 2003 Creative Teaching Press

The greedy python

was so hungry you see!

It _____ the gorilla,

And now it is after me!

The End

8

The greedy python was

so hungry you see!

It _____ the jaguar,

But it didn't _____ me!

7

Rain Forest Adventures © 2003 Creative Teaching Press

Independent Reading

Safari Sleep Over Fun

MATERIALS

✓ rain forest books
✓ rain forest stuffed animals
✓ safari guide items (i.e., flashlight, blanket, binoculars, "bug repellent"—spray bottle with water, hat)
✓ disposable camera
✓ backpack
✓ puffy paints

Write a parent letter to introduce the Safari Sleep Over Bag and explain how children will use its contents. (See sample letter below.) Or, photocopy the sample letter and sign your name. Place rain forest books and stuffed animals, safari guide items, and a disposable camera in a backpack. Use puffy paints to write *Safari Sleep Over Bag* on the backpack. Send home the letter and backpack with a different child each night. After every child has taken home the backpack, develop the photos, and use them to create a class book titled *Room _____'s Safari Sleep Over Fun!*

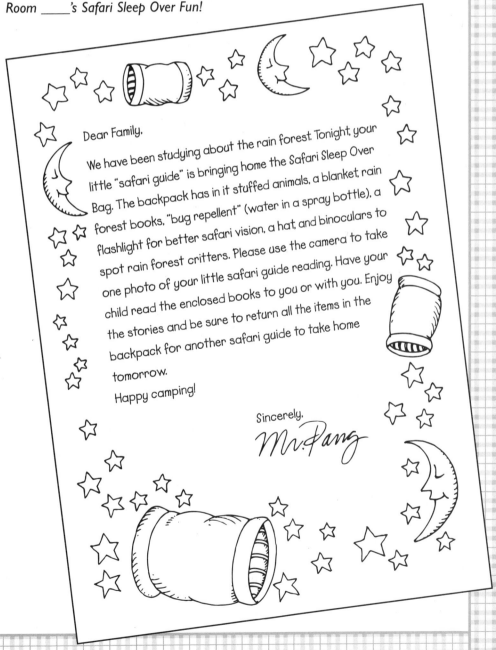

Dear Family,

We have been studying about the rain forest. Tonight, your little "safari guide" is bringing home the Safari Sleep Over Bag. The backpack has in it stuffed animals, a blanket, rain forest books, "bug repellent" (water in a spray bottle), a flashlight for better safari vision, a hat, and binoculars to spot rain forest critters. Please use the camera to take one photo of your little safari guide reading. Have your child read the enclosed books to you or with you. Enjoy the stories and be sure to return all the items in the backpack for another safari guide to take home tomorrow.

Happy camping!

Sincerely,

Mr. Pang

A Safari Guide's Adventure

Culminate your rain forest unit by inviting your little safari guides to perform a dramatic play that highlights what they learned. Make enough enlarged copies of the Props reproducible for every child to have a cutout. Give each child a Safari Guide's Adventure reproducible, and assign every child a part. (More than one child will have the same part.) There are five different characters: safari guides, gorillas, snakes, sloths, and macaws. Give each child an enlarged safari hat or animal cutout from the Props reproducible to color. Invite children to glue their hat or animal to a sentence strip to make a headband.

Place the transparency on the overhead projector, and project the scene onto a blank wall as the backdrop for the dramatic play. Read aloud the play on the Safari Guide's Adventure reproducible to introduce children to the characters and their lines. Have children practice their lines until they comfortably know them and are ready to perform in front of an audience of peers or parents.

MATERIALS

✓ Safari Guide's Adventure reproducible (page 29)
✓ Props reproducible (page 30)
✓ sentence strips
✓ color transparency of rain forest layers
✓ overhead projector
✓ art supplies

Safari Guide's Adventure

 Safari Guides: *(look at each other)* Safari guides look and see. What animal lives on the rain forest floor with me?

 Gorillas: *(enter)* We do!

 Safari Guides and Gorillas: *(look at guides)* Safari guides look and see. What animal lives in the understory?

 Snakes: *(slither in)* We do!

 Safari Guides, Gorillas, and Snakes: *(look at guides)* Safari guides look and see. What animal lives in the canopy?

 Sloths: *(slowly walk in)* We do!

 Safari Guides, Gorillas, Snakes, and Sloths: *(look at guides)* Safari guides look and see. What animal in the emergent layer looks down at me?

 Macaws: *(fly in)* We do!

 All Characters: Safari guides look and see how we all live together happily!

Rain Forest Adventures © 2003 Creative Teaching Press

Props

Rain Forest Adventures © 2003 Creative Teaching Press

Shared Writing

Rain Forest Word Bank

MATERIALS

✓ any animal reproducible (page 8, 10, 12, 30, 36, or 46)
✓ overhead transparency
✓ butcher paper
✓ construction paper
✓ colored markers

Create a rain forest word bank with your class. Use any animal reproducible in this book to make an overhead transparency. Project it onto a piece of butcher paper, trace it, and cut out the large rain forest animal. Have children help you spell names of rain forest animals and key words such as *rain, humid,* and *canopy.* Write each word in bold dark colors on a piece of construction paper, and cut it out in its lettered shape. (You can write vowels in a different color to help children identify them.) Glue these words (in alphabetical order or randomly) to the animal-shaped word bank you drew on butcher paper, and display it on a classroom wall for whole-class reference. Reread the word bank words for a daily shared reading experience. Remind children to refer to these words during independent, interactive, and shared writing activities.

Rain Forest Question of the Week

MATERIALS

✓ chart paper

Each week, write a different question about the rain forest at the top of a piece of chart paper. Read aloud the question, and model how to write the answer in a complete sentence. For example, if the question of the week is *What is your favorite rain forest animal?*, you might write *"I like the sloth best,"* said Mrs. Corcoran. Invite children to write their own sentence on the chart paper to answer the question during circle time, center time, or independent writing time. Encourage them to follow the frame you wrote as they write their own answer. Remind children to refer to the rain forest word bank (see above) and to use "temporary spelling" when they write their answer. This activity gives children the opportunity to write independently and use the writing strategies learned in class in a stress-free situation since they are choosing when during the week to add their answer to the chart paper. At the end of each week, invite the class to read with you the question and each child's answer. To extend the activity, make a class book called *The Rain Forest* with a page for each child. Write the question on the first page, and have children write their answer and draw an illustration on the following pages.

Meet the Safari Guides

MATERIALS

✓ Safari Guide reproducible (page 33)
✓ construction paper
✓ close-up photo of each child's face
✓ safari hat
✓ art supplies

Staple together several pieces of lined paper between two large sheets of construction paper to make a class book. Cut out a construction paper tree and jeep, and glue them on the front cover. Copy a class set of the Safari Guide reproducible, and glue a child's photo on each one. Each day, choose a different child to sit in a special chair and wear a safari hat. Ask children the same questions each day: *What is your favorite rain forest animal? Which layer of the rain forest does it live in?* Use the frame shown below to write children's responses on separate pages in the book. Ask children to help you sound out the words to spell them. Invite children to color their safari guide, cut it out, and glue it next to their responses in the class book. Each day, begin the activity by rereading the previous days' pages as shared reading.

> Meet Safari Guide Shayna.
> Her favorite animal is the sloth.
> It lives in the canopy of the rain forest.

Gorilla Facts and Fiction

MATERIALS

✓ *Gorillas: Gentle Giants of the Forest* by Joyce Milton
✓ *Willy the Wimp* by Anthony Browne
✓ sentence strips
✓ colored markers
✓ butcher paper
✓ art supplies

Read aloud *Gorillas: Gentle Giants of the Forest*, and invite children to share facts about gorillas. Write these facts on sentence strips. Read aloud *Willy the Wimp*, and invite children to share "fictional facts" about gorillas (e.g., Gorillas eat ice cream). Use a different colored marker to write these fictional facts on sentence strips. Draw a large gorilla on butcher paper (or enlarge the gorilla on the Props reproducible on page 30). On one side of the gorilla, add a hat or bow tie to make it look like a fictional character and write *Fiction* on its foot. Write *Fact* on the foot on its other side. Read aloud the sentences, and invite children to glue each sentence strip to the correct side of the gorilla. Invite children to reread the facts for shared reading.

Rain Forest Adventures © 2003 Creative Teaching Press

Interactive Writing

Write a Rhyme

MATERIALS

✓ sentence strips
✓ construction paper or butcher paper
✓ art supplies

Have children brainstorm names of rain forest animals. Then, have them brainstorm words that describe the animals and rhyme with the numbers in the poem shown below. Use interactive writing to have children write each line of the poem on a separate sentence strip. Invite volunteers to write a letter, a word chunk, a whole word, or punctuation for each line. Mount the sentence strips on large pieces of construction paper or butcher paper to make a Big Book. Invite children to paint or draw an illustration for each sentence, and attach it to the appropriate page. Bind together the pages, and use the class book for shared reading. To extend the activity, have children write lines of the poem up to the number 10.

> 1. 1 monkeys are _fun_
>
> 2. 2 jaguars aren't _blue_
>
> 3. 3 parrots live in a _tree_
>
> 4. 4 tigers _roar_
>
> 5. 5 bats _dive_
>
> 1, 2, 3, 4, 5 the rain forest is _alive!_

Did You Know?

MATERIALS

✓ chart paper
✓ construction paper

Use interactive writing to have children write *Did you know* on chart paper to begin a question. Then, invite a volunteer to share a fact about the rain forest (e.g., *There are more ants in the rain forest than any other creature*). Write the fact to complete the question, read aloud the question, and invite the volunteer to write his or her name next to it. Have the class repeat the process with another question. Once the class has several questions, type them, mount them on construction paper, and display them in the classroom or bind them into a class book for children to reread independently.

Guided Writing

Piranhas

MATERIALS

✓ *Piranhas* by Mary Berendes
✓ Piranha reproducible (page 36)
✓ white paper
✓ construction paper
✓ art supplies

Read aloud *Piranhas*, and discuss facts children learned. Give each child a Piranha reproducible. Invite children to use facts about piranhas to complete the sentence frame and write additional sentences. Encourage them to cut out their piranha, trace it on several pieces of white paper, and continue writing facts on these additional pages. Have children trace their piranha on construction paper, cut it out, and use art supplies to decorate the cutout to look like a piranha, including sharp teeth in its mouth. Staple children's writing behind their construction paper piranha, and use the piranhas for the Waterfall and Piranha Pond bulletin board display described on page 61.

In the Rain Forest

MATERIALS

✓ In the Rain Forest reproducible (page 37)
✓ green butcher paper
✓ white construction paper
✓ fishing line or curling ribbon
✓ art supplies

Cut a giant green butcher paper palm tree leaf for each child. Give each child an In the Rain Forest reproducible. Have children complete the sentence frame and then write additional sentences. For example, children can complete the sentence frame by writing *In the rain forest, Luca can climb like a monkey. He can swing from tree to tree. He likes to make noise as he climbs and swings*. Encourage children to extend their writing into a story and continue it on lined paper. Invite children to paint or draw a picture to illustrate their writing on white construction paper. Attach each child's writing and picture to a giant leaf (staple additional pages behind the reproducible). Display children's writing by hanging the leaves on fishing line in the classroom. Or, hole-punch each leaf, and use curling ribbon to bind together the leaves to create a Big Book that children can reread over and over again.

Piranha

_____'s piranha ate

_____

and _____ . So watch out for your

_____ !

Rain Forest Adventures © 2003 Creative Teaching Press

In the Rain Forest

In the rain forest,

_____ can

_____ like

a _____.

_____

_____

_____

_____

_____

Rain Forest Adventures © 2003 Creative Teaching Press

Independent Writing

Safari Guide

MATERIALS

✓ Safari Hat reproducible (page 39)
✓ small paper plates
✓ toilet paper rolls
✓ construction paper
✓ raffia
✓ art supplies

Tell children to pretend they are safari guides who will teach people about animals that live in the rain forest. Have children draw and paint a rain forest animal. Then, invite children to write facts about their animal in an acrostic poem. Have them write the name of their animal down the left side of a piece of lined paper with one letter on each line. On each line, have them write a word that describes the animal and begins with that letter. For a fun display, invite children to make a safari guide. Have them paint a paper plate and add hair and facial features. Then, have them color and cut out a Safari Hat reproducible, cut along the slit, and attach it to their paper-plate head. Invite them to sponge-paint an empty toilet paper roll, cut it in half, and glue the two halves over the safari guide's eyes as binoculars. Have children trace their hands on construction paper, cut them out, and staple the hand cutouts on the plate to make it look like they are holding the binoculars. Mount children's animal and writing on a sheet of construction paper, and tie it to their safari guide with raffia. Hang the safari guides around the classroom. Encourage children to read each other's animal facts for independent reading.

Safari Hat

Rain Forest Adventures © 2003 Creative Teaching Press

Marvelous Monkeys

MATERIALS

✓ construction paper
✓ art supplies

Prior to this activity, use shared writing to have children help you create a word bank about monkeys. Ask them to help you sound out and spell words that describe what monkeys look like, where they live, and how they act. Cut out a large tan or brown construction paper oval for each child. Have children write on their oval *Monkeys can* and then independently complete the sentence starter and write additional sentences about what monkeys can do. Encourage them to refer to the word bank as they write. Invite children to make a large construction paper monkey (see sample). Glue or staple children's writing to their monkey's body. Display the monkeys, and encourage children to read them independently.

Crocodile Facts

MATERIALS

✓ *Crocodiles Yawn to Keep Cool* by Kate Petty
✓ Crocodile reproducible (page 41)
✓ green construction paper
✓ egg cartons (half for each child)
✓ art supplies

Copy the Crocodile reproducible on green construction paper for each child, and cut it out. Read aloud *Crocodiles Yawn to Keep Cool* to introduce children to facts about crocodiles. Invite groups of children to meet with you to write facts they have learned about crocodiles. Ask children to share facts and details with the group. Have children write crocodile facts on strips of lined paper. Then, invite children to decorate their crocodile. Have children paint half an egg carton (the crocodile's bumpy back). Staple the egg carton to the back of the crocodile. Glue or staple children's writing to the underside of the crocodile's body. Invite children to read each other's facts independently.

Crocodile

Rain Forest Adventures © 2003 Creative Teaching Press

Math

Rain Forest Treat Tote

MATERIALS

✓ _____'s Family Food Graph (page 43)
✓ Treat Tote Family Letter (page 43)
✓ construction paper
✓ puffy paints
✓ backpack
✓ resealable plastic bags
✓ food items (for each child): 6 chocolate chips, 1 teaspoon (5 mL) of coconut, 6 peanuts, 6 banana chips
✓ books about the rain forest and food in the rain forest (see literature list on page 14)

Staple together a class set of copies of the _____'s Family Food Graph inside a construction paper cover to make a Rain Forest Treat Journal. Use puffy paints to decorate a backpack and write *Rain Forest Treats* on it. Copy the Treat Tote Family Letter, which explains what children will be doing with the backpack. Mount the letter on construction paper, laminate it, and attach it to the backpack. Place the journal, a bag of food items, and books in the backpack. Explain to children that they will each have a chance to take home the backpack. Tell children that they will read books about the rain forest and rain forest foods with their family. Then, they will taste four different foods that come from the rain forest and have up to five people in their family taste the foods. Then, they will fill out a graph to show which food each family member liked best and analyze the information on their completed graph. Send the backpack home with a different child each day. Have the child show his or her graph to the class and share the results the next day.

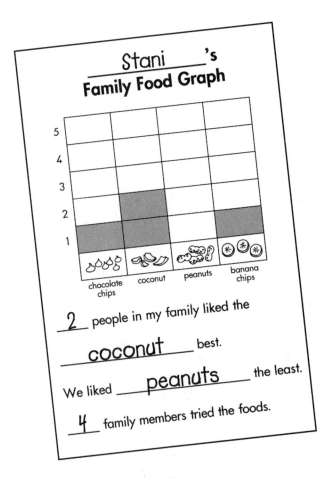

Family Food Graph

_____'s

	chocolate chips	coconut	peanuts	banana chips
5				
4				
3				
2				
1				

_____ people in my family liked the

We liked _____ best.

_____ the least.

_____ family members tried the foods.

Treat Tote Family Letter

Dear Family,

We have been learning about foods that come from the rain forest. Please read the enclosed books to or with your child.

Have each family member taste the foods in the bag and record his or her favorite food on the graph. Please help your child analyze the information and fill out the bottom of the graph. Please be sure to return the journal and books in the back-pack tomorrow for another safari guide to take home.

Happy safari snacking!

Sincerely,

_____

Rain Forest Adventures © 2003 Creative Teaching Press

Animal Quilt Glyph

MATERIALS

✓ Animal Glyph Key reproducible (page 45)
✓ Animal Heads reproducible (page 46)
✓ construction paper
✓ box
✓ marbles
✓ raffia
✓ art supplies

Copy the Animal Glyph Key reproducible, mount it on construction paper, and display it. Give each child an Animal Heads reproducible. Have children choose which rain forest animal from the reproducible they like best, cut it out, and mount it on a 9" (23 cm) black construction paper square. Then, have children add eyes to represent their favorite color and beak stripes, hair, spots, or stripes to represent their age according to the directions on the glyph key. Invite children to place a 9" yellow construction paper square in a box and roll marbles dipped in black paint on the paper to make a safari design. Invite children to help you hole-punch the corners of each square, and use raffia to connect the black and yellow squares in a pattern to create a "quilt." Display the quilt next to the glyph key. Have children use the key to analyze the data in each picture. For example, a child might say *Damon chose a snake so that is his favorite rain forest animal. His snake has green eyes so green must be his favorite color. There are six spots on the snake so Damon is six years old.*

Animal Glyph Key

1 <u>Which animal do you like best?</u>
Choose a toucan, a monkey, a snake, or a tiger.

2 <u>What is your favorite color?</u>
Color your animal's eyes the same color as your favorite color.

3 <u>How old are you?</u>
Cut out the same number of stripes and glue them on the **toucan**'s beak.

Cut out the same number of pieces of hair and glue them on the **monkey**'s head.

Cut out the same number of spots and glue them on the **snake**.

Cut out the same number of stripes and glue them on the **tiger**.

Rain Forest Adventures © 2003 Creative Teaching Press

Animal Heads

Rain Forest Adventures © 2003 Creative Teaching Press

Peanut Monkey Math

ⓂⒶⓉⒺⓡⒾⒶⓁⓢ

✓ construction paper
✓ white labels
✓ peanuts with shells
✓ ½" (13 mm) pipe cleaners
✓ art supplies

Give each child a piece of construction paper, and have children create a rain forest scene with at least one tree in it. Have children place a label on their paper. Choose a number, and give each child that many peanuts. Ask children to use a black marker to draw a face on each peanut and then glue a pipe cleaner "tail" to each one. For counting, have children count how many "monkeys" they have, glue them to their picture, and write the number on the label. For addition, have children glue the monkeys in two different places on their picture and write an addition equation on the label. For subtraction, have children place all their monkeys on their tree, move some monkeys to the ground, and write a subtraction equation on the label.

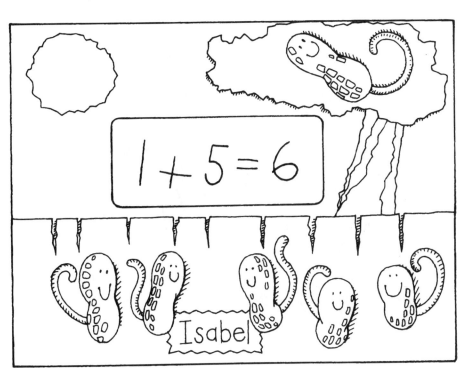

Interactive Monkey Math Poem

ⓂⒶⓉⒺⓡⒾⒶⓁⓢ

✓ "Banana Tree" poem (page 48)
✓ tagboard
✓ yellow construction paper
✓ Velcro®
✓ overhead marker

Make an enlarged copy of the poem "Banana Tree" on tagboard, and laminate it. Cut out ten yellow construction paper bananas, and laminate them. Use Velcro to attach the bananas to the tree. Ask the class to count how many bananas are in the tree. Then, read aloud the poem, and use an overhead marker to write a number in the blank. Remove that many bananas from the tree. Count how many bananas are left on the tree. Reread the poem several times, taking a banana or several bananas away each time. To extend the activity, have children write and solve a subtraction equation on a dry erase board to illustrate how many bananas started out on the tree and how many are removed.

Banana Tree

Way up high in a banana tree,

A hungry monkey smiled down at me!

I shook that tree as hard as I could.

Down came _____ bananas.

Mmm! They were good!

Rain Forest Adventures © 2003 Creative Teaching Press

Addition Tree Frog

MATERIALS

✓ construction paper
✓ black and white beans
✓ newspaper
✓ art supplies

Cut a class set of red construction paper strips (frog tongues), and give one to each child. Invite children to glue two different colors of beans (flies) to their "frog tongue" to create an addition equation (white beans + black beans). Invite children to make a frog. Have them sponge-paint dots on a piece of construction paper, draw a large oval on the paper, cut it out, and cut it in half to make two sides of the body. Staple the halves together, stuff them with newspaper, and attach arms and legs. Then, have children add a face and glue their tongue with flies to their frog. Write on the board _____'s frog ate __ white flies and __ black flies, and write ____ + ____ = ____. Have children copy the frames on a piece of paper and fill in the blanks about their own frog. Or, type the sentence frame and make a copy for each child to complete. Have children glue their paper to the back of their frog.

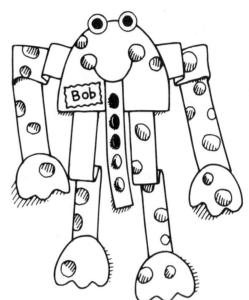

Beetle Bug Clock

MATERIALS

✓ The Grouchy Ladybug by Eric Carle
✓ Clock Bug Body reproducible (page 50)
✓ construction paper
✓ small paper plates
✓ brass fasteners
✓ art supplies

Copy a class set of the Clock Bug Body reproducible on construction paper. Have children cut out their bug body, paint a paper plate, and cut the plate in half to create wings. Have them staple the wings to the back of their bug body and add spots, eyes, and legs. Use brass fasteners to attach each child's clock hands to his or her bug body. Read aloud *The Grouchy Ladybug*, and have children move the hands on their clock to match the times in the book. Invite children to hold up their clock so you can check that they have the correct time. Have a volunteer say what time the clocks are showing. To extend the activity, have children use spots to create an addition equation on their bug's wings. For example, a child could put seven spots on the left wing and four on the right wing and write and solve the equation 7 + 4 = 11.

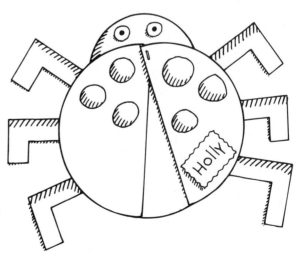

Clock Bug Body

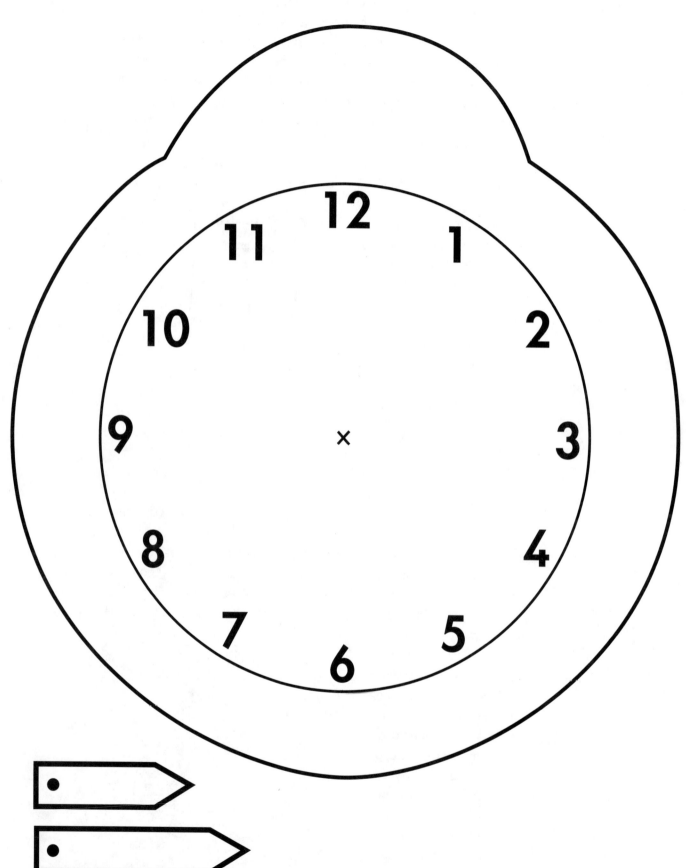

Rain Forest Adventures © 2003 Creative Teaching Press

Science

Camouflage Tree Frogs

M A T E R I A L S

✓ construction paper
✓ newspaper
✓ timer
✓ rain forest animal puppets

Cut out the same number of frog shapes from various colors of construction paper and from newspaper. Or, trace frog-shaped cutouts. Discuss how animals protect themselves. Put sheets of newspaper on the floor, and put the frogs on them. Tell children to pretend they are hungry rain forest animals who are looking for dinner. Set the timer for 1 minute, and tell children to use a puppet to pick up as many frogs as they can. Record how many of each color frog children picked up. Discuss what color frogs were picked up the most and the least and why. Less newspaper frogs should have been picked up because they were the most camouflaged. Discuss how camouflage is the only source of protection many animals have in a rain forest filled with hungry predators. To extend the activity, invite children to create a picture with a camouflaged animal hiding in the rain forest.

Plant a Jungle Garden

M A T E R I A L S

✓ grass seed
✓ large pot
✓ soil
✓ chart paper
✓ plastic cups
✓ construction paper
✓ close-up photo of each child's face
✓ skewers or dowels
✓ art supplies

Plant grass seed (Winter Rye grows quickly) in a large pot of soil. Ask children to monitor the growth of the grass in the large pot. When children observe a change, record it on chart paper. Invite a volunteer to document the change by drawing the pot and plant on the chart paper and recording the date below the drawing. Invite children to plant their own grass seed. Poke a hole in the bottom of a plastic cup for each child. Have children add soil and grass seed to their cup. To add a safari look to the plants, have children draw a safari jeep and a flower with the face of a rain forest animal (e.g., toucan tulip, tiger lily, parrot pansy) on it on construction paper. Glue children's photos in the driver's seat of their jeep, and attach it to the front of their cup. Glue each flower to a skewer or dowel, and have children put it in their cup.

Rain Forest Birds Like to Eat

MATERIALS

✓ *Rainforest Birds* by Bobbie Kalman

✓ Bird Food Cards (page 53)

✓ What Do Rain Forest Birds Eat? reproducible (page 54)

✓ resealable plastic bags

✓ set of tools for each group (coffee stirrer, pliers, tweezers)

✓ set of food for each group (assorted nuts, gummy bugs, cup of sugar water, birdseed, sunflower seeds, cup of orange juice)

Copy the Bird Food Cards for each small group of children. Copy a class set of the What Do Rain Forest Birds Eat? reproducible. Cut apart the food cards, and put each set in a plastic bag. Make a copy of the birds at the bottom of this page, cut out the birds, and tape each one to the tool that is most similar to its beak: hummingbird to a coffee stirrer, macaw to pliers, and quetzal to tweezers. Discuss with the class what tools children use to eat (e.g., fork, spoon, chopsticks, hands) and why they use different tools to eat different foods. Read aloud *Rainforest Birds*, and discuss what birds eat and how they eat it. Ask children what kinds of food birds can pick up with their beaks. Show them pictures of the three birds for this activity and the food cards. Display an enlarged copy of the What Do Rain Forest Birds Eat? reproducible. Ask children to hypothesize which birds will be able to pick up each food shown on the cards. Tape each food card in the appropriate column.

Give each child a What Do Rain Forest Birds Eat? reproducible. Give each group a bag of food cards, a set of tools, and a set of food. Have groups use the different tools to see which "beak" works best for picking up each food. Have each child glue each food card under the bird that can best eat the food with its beak. Have children compare their completed charts and discuss why each bird can and cannot pick up each food item. Invite children to look at the results of their investigation and compare them to the class's hypotheses.

Bird Food Cards

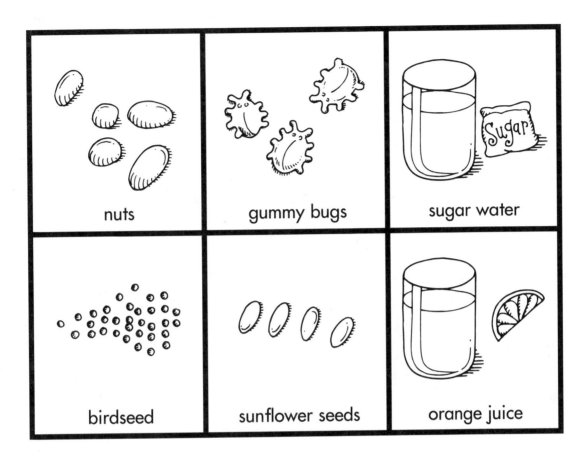

nuts   gummy bugs   sugar water

birdseed   sunflower seeds   orange juice

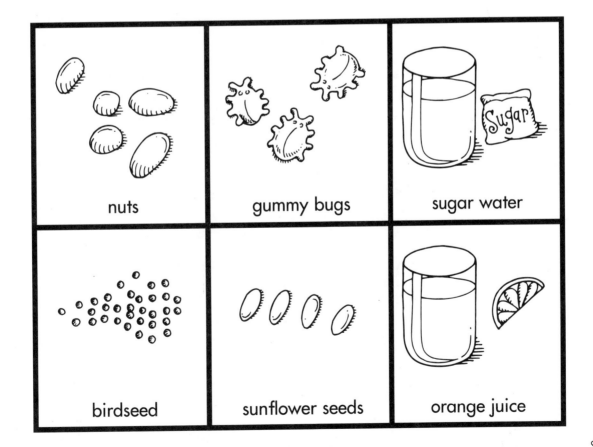

nuts   gummy bugs   sugar water

birdseed   sunflower seeds   orange juice

Rain Forest Adventures © 2003 Creative Teaching Press

What Do Rain Forest Birds Eat?

hummingbird	macaw	quetzal

Rain Forest Adventures © 2003 Creative Teaching Press

Social Studies

Rain Forest Guessing Bucket

MATERIALS

✓ *How Monkeys Make Chocolate: Foods and Medicines from the Rainforests* by Adrian Forsyth

✓ Guessing Bucket Family Letter (page 56)

✓ plastic bucket with lid

Copy the Guessing Bucket Family Letter, and attach it to a bucket. Read aloud *How Monkeys Make Chocolate: Foods and Medicines from the Rainforests*. Discuss the products that come from the rain forest and their importance. Decorate the bucket with vines, trees, and rain forest products, and write *Rain Forest Guessing Fun* on the lid. Each day, choose a different child to take home the bucket, put a rain forest product in it, and write three clues about the product. On the following day, have the child share the clues and challenge the class to identify the product. Have the child who correctly identifies the product take home the bucket that evening. Invite the class to discuss the importance of the item in the bucket, how it was grown or made, and what effects its disappearance may have on the world.

Rain Forest People

MATERIALS

✓ *People in the Rain Forest* by Saviour Pirotta

✓ construction paper

✓ art supplies

Read aloud *People in the Rain Forest*. Discuss the lives of the people in the book. Ask children how their own lives are similar to and different from people who live in the rain forest. Record children's answers on a chart. Divide the class into pairs. Invite each pair to fold a large piece of construction paper in half and paint a picture of life in the rain forest and a picture of their life that illustrates a similarity or difference between the ways people live in the two different places. For example, children might paint a picture of a person hunting for meat in the rain forest and one of their mom buying meat at a store. Cut out a hut-shaped piece of construction paper for each pair, glue their pictures to it, and bind pages together to make a class book. To extend the activity, have children independently write sentences that describe the similarities and differences in the two cultures. Invite children to share their pictures with the class and explain the similarity or difference they illustrated.

People of the rain forest hunt animals to get meat.

My family buys meat at the food store.

Guessing Bucket Family Letter

Dear Family,

We have been learning about the rain forest and how it provides us with many important products. Please help your child add to our bucket something that comes from the rain forest. Then, help your child write three clues that describe the product. Tomorrow, your child will share the clues with our class to see if we can identify the item. Use the following list of rain forest products to help you choose an item for the bucket:

cucumber	cinnamon	tea	coffee
ginger	nutmeg	orange	lemon
sweet potato	grapefruit	cocoa	chewing gum
vanilla	cashews	banana	avocado
pineapple	sugar cane	rice	peanuts

If you do not have anything on the list, have your child draw a picture of a product. Please return the bucket with the product and clues in it tomorrow so another Rain Forest Detective can have a turn.

Thank you,

Rain Forest Adventures © 2003 Creative Teaching Press

Save the Rain Forest Bookmaking

MATERIALS

✓ *Recycle! A Handbook for Kids* by Gail Gibbons or *Where Does the Garbage Go?* by Paul Showers

✓ potato chip bags, newspapers, cereal boxes

✓ small metal rings

✓ art supplies

Read aloud *Recycle! A Handbook for Kids* or *Where Does the Garbage Go?* Discuss with the class what reusing and recycling are and why they are important. Discuss what household products come from the rain forest and why many rain forests are becoming endangered. Explain that people can help save the rain forests by recycling and reusing. Make books from recycled materials as described below or other materials that children think of. Invite children to write about what people can do to save the rain forests or how people can reuse and recycle to help the environment. Make awards from reused materials, and present them to children who reuse and recycle.

Potato Chip Bags

Make book covers from potato chip bags (lunch-size or family-size bags). Cut three sides of the bags and staple paper inside. Have children write a story and illustrate it.

Newspapers

Give children several pages of newspaper. Have them cut the pages into any size and staple the pages together to form a book. Invite children to use a marker to write a story on the newspaper (so it will show up and be readable on the newsprint). Or, have children make a "newspaper book" and then search on a separate newspaper page to find specific letters. Tell them to cut out the letters, glue each letter to a separate square of white paper, and glue each square to a page in their book. For example, have children find all the letters of their name and glue each letter on a different page.

Cereal Boxes

Cut the front and back off a cereal box to form a book cover. Use small metal rings to bind lined paper inside the cover. Invite children to write a story in their book.

Culminating Event and Extra Fun

At the end of your unit, invite children and their families to visit the classroom so children can act as a safari guide to show off all the projects they completed during the unit and share the information they learned about the rain forest. Arrange your classroom so all the projects children completed are displayed. Prior to the event, have children practice leading a partner or small group around the classroom and explaining each project. This will help prepare children and make them feel confident when their family visits the classroom. Invite children to complete the following fun activities to provide decorations and props for the "big event."

Rain Forest Invitation

MATERIALS

✓ Rain Forest Invitation (page 62)
✓ 12" x 18" (30.5 cm x 46 cm) sheets of construction paper
✓ art supplies

Give each child a Rain Forest Invitation to complete. Show children how to fold a sheet of construction paper so the two sides meet in the middle to make "doors." Have children unfold their paper and glue their invitation in the middle of it. Invite children to decorate the doors with vines, leaves, and rain forest animals.

Binoculars

MATERIALS

✓ toilet paper rolls (2 per child)
✓ curling ribbon
✓ art supplies

Have each child paint a camouflage design on two toilet paper rolls. Staple together each child's rolls to make "binoculars." Hole-punch each roll, and insert curling ribbon to make a cord.

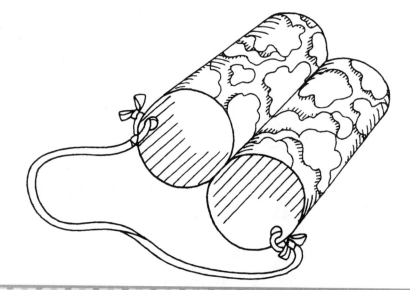

Safari Sack

MATERIALS

✓ brown grocery bags with handles
✓ white construction paper
✓ art supplies

Type a label for each child that says _____'s *Safari Sack*. Have each child sponge-paint a camouflage design on both sides of a bag. Invite children to draw a rain forest animal on white construction paper, cut it out, and glue it on their bag. Have children write their name on their label and glue it on their bag. At the end of the rain forest unit, have children carry their work home in their sack.

The Large Python

MATERIALS

✓ butcher paper
✓ newspaper
✓ photo of each child's face
✓ construction paper
✓ yarn
✓ art supplies

Invite the class to make a python. Have children paint a large sheet of butcher paper and use sponges to add spots. Fold the paper in half, and cut it in the shape of a snake. Glue together the sides, and stuff newspaper inside the snake. Glue children's photos on a red forked tongue, and attach it to the python's mouth. Have children use interactive writing to help you make a construction paper sign that says *Munch! Crunch! Munch! Crunch! I eat Kindergartners [First Graders] for lunch.* Use yarn to hang the sign around the python's neck. Display the python in the classroom.

Munch! Crunch! Munch! Crunch! I eat Kindergartners for lunch.

Yummy Food Recipes

MATERIALS

✓ Piranha Ponds Recipe (page 63)
✓ Jungle Juice Recipe (page 64)

Gather for each child the ingredients, materials, and measuring tools listed on a recipe. Give each child a copy of the recipe. Have children follow the recipe, color each illustration, and fill in the appropriate information as needed. For the Piranha Ponds recipe, mix blue food coloring with cream cheese before giving ingredients to children. Have children choose how many piranha they want to add in step 3.

Large Rain Forest Tree

MATERIALS

✓ bucket of sand
✓ boxes with lids (e.g., boxes that hold reams of paper)
✓ masking tape
✓ butcher paper
✓ fishing line
✓ art supplies

Place a bucket of sand in a box, and place the lid on it. Stack several more boxes on top, and use masking tape to tape them together to make a "tree trunk." Cover the boxes with brown butcher paper. Fold several yards (meters) of brown butcher paper in half, and cut it. Wrinkle the paper, and then wrap it around the trunk to create "bark." Sponge-paint the trunk brown and green to add a textured look. Twist brown butcher paper, and staple it to the top of the trunk to create "branches." Hang fishing line from the ceiling, and connect it to the branches so they stand up. Sponge-paint green butcher paper with several shades of green paint. Cut the paper into the shape of large leaves, and staple the "leaves" to the branches.

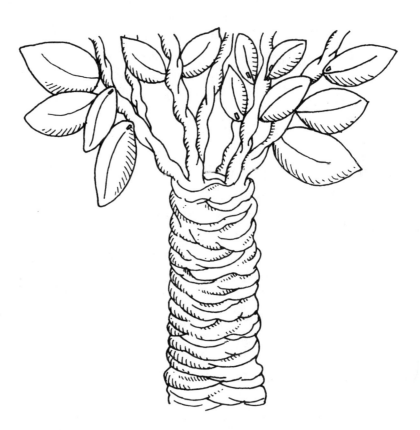

Safari Snack Shack

MATERIALS

✓ cardboard appliance box or premade playhouse
✓ grass skirts and bamboo or brown butcher paper and raffia
✓ palm leaves or elephant ear plant leaves
✓ table and tablecloth with a safari-related design

Build a cardboard playhouse from an appliance box, or use one you already have in your classroom. Hang grass skirts from the side of the playhouse, and wrap bamboo around the outside of it. Or, use brown butcher paper to cover the sides and then add raffia to create a safari look. Lay leaves on the roof. Add a table and a tablecloth, and invite children to eat in the Safari Snack Shack. (Integrate math by giving children menus and having them order and pay for food.)

Sunset Jungle Cruise Bulletin Board

MATERIALS

✓ Safari Hat reproducible (page 39)
✓ butcher paper
✓ blue cellophane
✓ small paper plates
✓ construction paper
✓ string
✓ rain forest animal stickers
✓ art supplies

Cut out two or three (depending on your class size) canoe-shaped butcher paper boats. Make a red and white striped butcher paper awning for each boat. Display the boats on a bulletin board. Then, add cellophane for "water." Ask children to paint a paper plate and add a face. Have children color and cut out a Safari Hat reproducible and then slide it over their paper-plate "head." Invite children to make a construction paper camera and use string to attach it to their paper-plate head. Have them place an animal sticker on the lens of their camera. Attach the heads to the boats on the bulletin board, and add various rain forest animals. Use interactive writing to have children write captions for the things they see on their "jungle cruise," and place them on the display. For example, children could write *Look, a snake!* or *Watch out for the monkeys.*

Waterfall and Piranha Pond Bulletin Board

MATERIALS

✓ butcher paper
✓ newspapers
✓ art supplies

Have the class sponge-paint two large pieces of black butcher paper to create a rocky texture. Cover a bulletin board with blue butcher paper, and attach the "rocky" paper to form a waterfall on either end of the board. Stuff newspaper behind the waterfalls. Invite children to paint waves or water with various shades of blue paint. Staple the completed piranhas from the Piranhas activity on page 35 in the pond.

Rain Forest Invitation

Dear Family,

We have been learning about the rain forest.
We are very excited to share the rain forest
with you! Please join us.

Date: _____

Time: _____

Place: _____

Love,
Safari Guide

_____

Please wear safari or tropical attire

Rain Forest Adventures © 2003 Creative Teaching Press

Piranha Ponds Recipe

by Chef _____

Ingredients: food coloring, cream cheese,
graham cracker, fish crackers

Materials: small paper plate, plastic knife

1 Take 1 graham cracker.

2 Spread on blue cream cheese to make water.

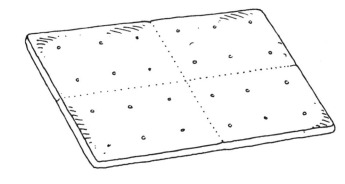

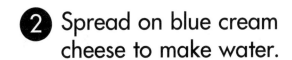

3 Add _____ piranha (fish crackers) to your water.

4 Eat them up before they eat you!

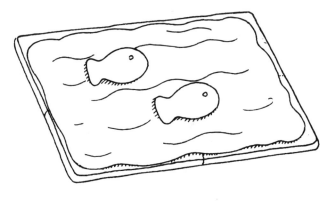

Rain Forest Adventures © 2003 Creative Teaching Press

Jungle Juice Recipe

by Chef _____

Ingredients: orange, lemon, water, sugar, banana, grapes, ice cubes

Materials: paper cup, plastic knife, skewer

Measuring tools: $\frac{1}{2}$ cup, teaspoon

1 Squeeze $\frac{1}{2}$ orange into a cup. Squeeze $\frac{1}{4}$ lemon into the cup.

2 Add $\frac{1}{2}$ cup water. Add 1 teaspoon of sugar. Stir.

3 Cut $\frac{1}{2}$ banana into slices. Make a pattern of bananas and grapes on a skewer.

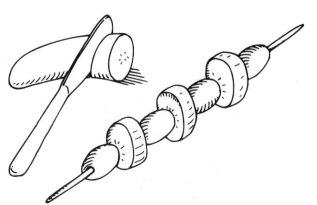

4 Add ice to the cup. Stir your Jungle Juice with your skewer. Drink and enjoy!

Rain Forest Adventures © 2003 Creative Teaching Press